I0423525

Assertive Communication Skills

Gain Respect Through Assertive And Decisive Behavior

Table of Contents

Introduction

I want to thank you and congratulate you for purchasing the book, *"Be More Assertive: How to Make Yourself Heard and Gain Respect through Assertiveness and Decisive Action"*.

This book contains proven steps and strategies on how to become more self-confident and assertive in order to succeed in both your career and personal relationships. The tips and examples in this book are very valuable in helping you change the way you play the game of life, so you can come out a winner. You will also learn helpful techniques on how to improve the way you think, act and sound, so you can make yourself heard and ultimately gain the respect of the people around you.

Thanks again for purchasing this book. I hope you enjoy it!

Chapter 1: Change the Way You Play the Game

Stop pretending that life is not a game.

Whether you accept it or not, life is indeed a game that has its own regulations, limits, losers and winners. Some people have the tendency to approach life as if it were a fund-raiser, picnic or concert where they expect everyone to act nicely. Of course, you would always prefer win-win situations, but eventually you will experience situations where you end up as the loser. Seeing life as a game does not necessarily mean that you will wish loss or failure on everyone else. Rather, it means that life is competitive. It shows that you are familiar with its rules, and you create your own strategies to make those rules work to your benefit.

Sometimes, when you aim to always be polite and laid-back in dealing with other people, those people may view you as frail and indecisive. In the end, you do not get the kind of life you wish for yourself and your family and you feel frustrated.

What you need to understand is that life is not a simple game. The rules actually change from situation to situation. What works with a particular situation will not necessarily work with another one. You always need to keep your eye on the ball, so you can become a winner and live your dream life.

Here are some useful tips you can try to better understand the importance of seeing life as a game:

You can study how to play the game of chess which can aid you in developing a more tactical or strategic mindset.

Look for a possible mentor who you can trust and look up to. Look for someone who is already successful in life and who will be willing to share his or her wisdom with you.

If you are not presently playing any sport, it is a good idea to start now. It does not really matter what sport you choose. You can play badminton, bowling or golf. The aim is for you to better understand how to play a game and strategize to win.

Stop being naive.

We have been taught to give people the benefit of the doubt. Sometimes we get caught in the trap of taking what other people say at face value. We normally do not want to investigate deeply to see if what we were told is true, because we want to trust the other person and avoid humiliating him or her. When we rigidly focus on our daily tasks, we normally overlook the more apparent behaviors of the people around us.

Realize that when you allow your naiveté to get out of hand, you can actually get into trouble. When you choose to turn your back on the bad things that other people do, you can only make things worse until your problems have become so big that they become difficult to resolve.

It is very common for people to see naiveté in another person as invigorating and stimulating. There are a lot of instances when younger people, who are only starting their careers, gain from their naiveté, because they are able to attract mentors who want to help them succeed in their careers. On the other hand, when naiveté is seen in older people, it can be used against those people to disgrace or shame them. Your expression of naiveté can underscore your incompetence in reading a situation properly or learning from your experiences. Here are useful tips on how you can overcome your naiveté.

- If there are things that do not seem sensible to you, you need to seek an explanation. If someone denies your request for an explanation, start being suspicious about his or her motives and intentions.

- Without imagining the worst-case scenario, you need to get in the habit of probing what other people's motives and intentions may be.

- Do not completely depend on the expertise of only one person when you are deciding on major issues. It is ideal to ask for opinions and advice from a number of reliable and trustworthy sources.

- When everyone agrees that something can't be done but you beg to differ, take some time out to think. When you know that you can make it work or there are things that can be done to make it work, take it as a sign that you may be becoming naive about the issue.

- Trust your own instincts.

Do not wait to be given what you want.

It is very common to hear people complaining and being disappointed because their needs have gone unmet. Although, when you take a closer look, you will see that these people did not actually ask for what they needed. Perhaps, they have not heard of the adage "The squeaky wheel gets the grease".

There are also people at the other end of the spectrum. These are the people who are never satisfied, no matter what they have been given, and other people end up defying their persistent requests.

Then there are those who were made to feel like they are demanding too much when they are actually not. If you do not ask for what you need or want, you do not risk hearing no, but you will also not get what you need or want.

If you believe that you deserve something, do not wait for other people to give it to you. Be bold and brave enough to ask for it. Here are useful tips you can use to be able to do this:

- Prepare your requests mentally ahead of time. Ponder on the things that you need and want and your reasons for needing and wanting them. When you ask for them, be forthright and sincere and supply a couple of reasons why you deserve to be given what you are asking for.

- Think about the benefit of employing "fait accompli," which is an effective technique in negotiations. The technique requires you to express your request in a statement form. For instance, instead of saying "I would like to ask for a two-week vacation to visit my family abroad who I have not seen in five years", you can say "I will be taking a two-vacation next month to visit my family abroad who I have not seen in five years. I have already made a turn-over plan for the tasks that I will be leaving behind."

- It is ideal if you can take classes on negotiation skills or you can read books about the topic so you will learn more effective techniques for use during negotiations.

- Disconnect being liked by other people from obtaining what you truly deserve, because these two things are mutually exclusive.

- Prudently select the right timing for voicing your requests. Asking for vacation time when everyone is busy finishing off backlogs is not a good idea. Always remember that timing is everything in life.

Do not avoid politics.

Attempting to avoid politics in the workplace is akin to attempting to avoid the weather. Whether you accept it or not, politics is a part of life. It is through politics that goals are accomplished, whether it is in the government, in the workplace or in any professional organization. If you do not involve yourself in the politics in your workplace, it only means that you are choosing to not play the game, and if you are not playing the game, it can only mean that you have very low chances of winning.

Politics is simply a matter of relationships. When you involve yourself in politics, it means that you understand the value of quid pro quo or "something in exchange of something else," which is integral to all relationships. Whatever profession you may be in, you should know that your career can be made or broken depending on the relationships that you maintain. When you realize that you need a particular relationship to move ahead in your career, chances are that it is already too late for you to build it. You need to realize that you should be building relationships continuously and with various types of people.

A successful relationship in your workplace, whether it is with your superior or with a colleague, is one wherein there is a clear definition of what you have to offer and what your expectations are from the other person. This is actually happening to a lot of people without them realizing it. Look at your relationship with a close friend. You may sometimes need advice from your friend, want his or her company as a shopping partner, need a golf buddy or a number of different things. If your friend is able to give you what you need, you are more willing to give the things that your friend needs or wants. You may not discuss these things with your friend beause the exchange is already implied in your friendship. Politics in the workplace functions the same way. Every time you make the effort to give someone something that he or she needs, you earn a symbolic "chip" that you can cash in in the future when you need that person to give you something.

Here are useful tips you can do to better play the game of politics:

- Handle political situations like you would any other negotiations. Spend some time in determining what the other party needs, what you have to offer, and how both of you can arrive at a win-win solution.

- Always remember the quid pro quo of politics, which means that something is always exchanged for something in return. Do not simply give in when other people ask something from you. Always think of what you would want to have in return. Do not be afraid to ask for what you deserve.

- Normally, you will gain in the long-term when you give up the smaller, less significant items. You can simply wait for the perfect time when you really need to cash in on the chips that you have earned.

- Do not avoid a situation you see as a political issue. When you do so, others will simply go around you. Handle political issues in a manner that allows other people to view you as a problem solver instead of a problem creator.

Do not hold your tongue.

When you fear being accused of acting too aggressive or pushy, you will normally stop yourself from saying ideas that are meant to be shared. Have you ever experienced withholding your comments only to have other people be admired for stating exactly what you wanted to say? Always remember that the accusation of being too aggressive is intended to shut you up. They are simple schemes to make you feel bad about owning your opinions and having a different viewpoint from other people. When you hold your tongue, you only increase your chances of becoming frustrated in the end, while appearing less enthusiastic than you truly are because you did not speak your thoughts.

Remember, you do not have to be rude when voicing your opinion. You can always find a good way to share your thoughts without actually becoming aggressive. As the saying goes, "disagree without being disagreeable." The best way to do this is to first acknowledge what the other party has done or said and then share your comment or opinion. A sample statement could be: "If I grasped your viewpoint accurately, you believe that this task should be transferred to our department. I suggest we sit down together to think about all the options to make sure that our processes are both optimized". Make sure you are well-prepared to back up your opinions with two or three valid justifications.

You can actually counter your feelings of being very pushy by adding an inquiry after you have voiced out your comments or opinions. For instance, you could say, "That is how I understand the situation. I am curious to hear what you think."

Chapter 2: Change the Way You Act

Your success greatly depends on whether you understand your role and how you need to play it. You may think that changing the way you act makes you pretentious or fake, but that is simply not true. We all know that an actor or an actress is evaluated based on how good he or she is in playing the given roles. The same is true for us, because we are all evaluated based on how we professionally act in our own chosen fields.

This chapter will focus on the subtle and conventional ways that a meek or timid person behaves that adds to the general impression of their being less capable and smart than they truly are. Any of the behaviors alone are not deal breakers, but when you put a couple of them together, they can easily reveal your fundamental gullibility, need for appreciation and lack of self-esteem.

Don't take polls before making decisions.

If you are very competent in the work that you do, but you are not willing or not able to make decisions without asking for inputs from everybody first, you may be viewed as incompetent by other people. Asking for opinions before making a decision is a common technique used by people who wish to avoid being confronted later on. They think if they can get everybody's approval from the start, they will no longer receive any criticisms later on. Yet, there really is a fine line between being viewed as a lone ranger who gives no value to other people's opinion and a weakling who cannot decide on his or her own. The ideal action is to act in an interdependent manner where you recognize that other people's inputs have their own merits, but you make the final decision based on your own judgment.

Stop needing to be liked.

There is no doubt that likability is a vital element that can spell your success. You can be promoted to a higher position or demoted to a lower one depending on your likability. You are also hired based on your likability, but you can also be fired because of it. All of us have this innate desire to be liked by other people and that desire is not wrong at all. However, when that want turns into an all-consuming need to be liked, it starts to outshine your rationality and sensibility, and it can get you in trouble.

Some people experience such a great need to be liked that it becomes almost impossible for them to act in a different way. Realize that there is a big difference between being liked by other people and being respected by them. If your sole concern is to be liked by other people, you have a high likelihood of not gaining other people's respect. Because of your great need to be liked, you will probably not take the precise risks that can gain the respect of other people. On the contrary, if your sole concern is to be respected by other people, you may end up losing the backing and support of other people who you may need to achieve your goals. Your goal should be to be both liked and respected so you can increase your chances of success.

To offset your desire to have everybody like you all the time, you can try the self-talk technique. You can talk to yourself and say your valid reasons for doing what you have deemed necessary. Also investigate the root causes of your excessive desire to be liked by other people. Find ways to balance your tendency to serve the needs of other people with attending to your own needs. Before you agree to do something you do not want to do, determine the implications if you do not do the task and the other party ends up a little bit annoyed. Always remember that when another person becomes angry or upset with you, it is because they have failed to control you. Do not fall for this scheme.

Do not be afraid to ask questions even if you think you will sound stupid.

Have you ever heard of the saying "There is no such thing as a stupid question?" You probably have but may put more trust in the saying "It is better to keep your mouth shut and look like a fool than to open it and remove all doubt." I do not agree with the second saying. When you ask a valid question to make sure that you fully understand the situation, you appear more self-confident than ignorant.

Sometimes, a person chooses to not ask a question, so he will not waste the time of other people. Here is one question you can ask yourself to assess whether your question deserves to be asked or not: "Will the answer to my question only be applicable to me?" If you answer yes, you can postpone asking the question at a later time. However, if you answer no or you know that you will not be able to ask the question again in the immediate future, then go head and ask. Do keep in mind the needs of other people. If you can sense that the other person cannot really attend to your question, decide how vital it is for you to obtain the answer from that person at that moment.

Here are some useful tips for you:

- If you don't understand anything, do not hesitate to ask. It is always better to ask instead of going around in circles because you do not know the right direction to go.

- When you are in a meeting, be observant of the other people to see if anyone else is confused. You can use this as your chance to get everyone on the same page by posing a question. Here is a sample of what you can say: "I noticed that some of us, including myself, are quite confused with the explanation you have just given. Can you provide us with a few examples so we can better understand?"

- Always trust your own instinct. If something appears to be unclear to you, it probably is.

- To clarify something, you can opt to make a simple paraphrase of what the other party has just explained. Here is an example: "Please tell me if my understanding is correct. You are giving us three months to finish the first phase of the new project, another three months to finish the second phase and just one month to finish the last phase." If your understanding is wrong, it will be a good opportunity for the other party to make any necessary clarifications.

- If someone makes you feel stupid for asking questions, that is the other person's problem and not yours. If you notice that that person has been consistently doing that, you can frankly ask his reasons for putting you down because you asked questions.

Do not be very concerned about upsetting or offending other people.

Here is a secret I will share with you: appearing offended or upset is a common ploy used by some people against a person gullible enough to believe it. When another person acts offended by what you have just said or done, there is an implication that what you have just said or done is inappropriate. Because of that, you may have the tendency to back down. When you frequently concede to other people, you are actually training other people to pretend being offended can be used to control you. In the end, you end up a loser.

A good technique you can use to avoid upsetting or offending another person when you wish to express a controversial point of view is to contrast what you actually want against what you do not want. Here is an example: "I do not wish to make it seem like I do not understand your point of view because I really do. But I wish to state another opinion about the matter."

You can also give a cautionary statement to the other person to inform him or her that what you are going to say is also difficult for you. Here is an example: "This is also quite hard for me to say but I wish to share with you my opinions about the issue." This statement will cue to other person to extend some patience with you.

If you believe you have voiced out your opinions without being offensive but the other party still takes offense, do not yield. Instead, react by simply acknowledging the other party's feelings. You can say "I think you have been offended by what I have just said..." and then listen to what the other party has to say. Stop yourself from backpedalling and negating your real opinions.

Chapter 3: Change the Way You Think

Altering how you think is very important to changing your self-defeating behaviors. Many people hold ideas about certain behaviors that will and will not gain them respect from others. These are referred to as "superstitious behaviors," because people believe that if they do not do those things, disastrous things can happen to them. Here are some examples: "I need to work harder compared to other people so I will be rewarded" or "I will be fired if I tell my boss what I really think about his ideas." Some of these beliefs may have been true in the past, but many of them are no longer applicable in our modern society. In the same way, these thoughts and behaviors may be beneficial to us when we were just starting in our careers, but they normally lose value as we gain more experience.

The attention and respect that an entry-level employee receives greatly depends on how he performs his or her tasks. If you are already hold a managerial or other leadership position, the respect that you receive depends instead on the behavior that you exhibit. You need work on your leadership and inter-personal skills. If these limiting beliefs worked for you when you were younger, you may find it difficult to give them up now that you hold a higher position. The lessons in this chapter will help you give up these beliefs that are holding you back.

Do not always take full responsibility.

Just because you have been given the role of project manager, it does not mean that you are the only person who can complete the project. Even if you can complete the project, it does not mean that you should do it all on your own. Being a leader simply means that you are responsible for making sure that your goals are achieved. You will not get much respect from other people when you try to complete a project all on your own. Actually, you may even gain more respect when other people see that you are capable of delegating tasks to your team members or you are able to influence them to perform well. This will show that you have what it takes to become a leader. When you engage other stakeholders into your project, you gain their trust at the onset and you could benefit from their wisdom, energy and other resources.

Here are some tips on how you can avoid taking full responsibility when you do not really have to:

- When you have been given a managerial or leadership role, prevent yourself from immediately "doing" something. Allow yourself to spend some time to think your task through so you will be able to plan your actions, identify the things you need to succeed, and so on.

- Be persistent in building relationships with everyone in your organization and in your own professional community. As I have mentioned in the previous chapter, when you think that you need a particular relationship, it is often too late for you to build it.

- Always remind yourself that you do not need to reinvent the wheel. In our modern world, almost everything has already been done by other people. If you need to complete a particular task, it could often mean that others have already done it before you. What you need to do is to look for those people and seek their guidance and expertise, so you can complete your task.

- Learn how to delegate. Distributing tasks to people who work under you will reduce your stress and workload, free you up to do more important work and gain you respect from the people around you.

Do not follow instructions obediently.

There are some people who change character when they are given instructions or assignments. They become so eager to complete the assignment as fast as they can that they miss opportunities to work smarter. They have the tendency to look at the details without seeing the bigger picture. You need to realize that those who succeed know how to strike a balance between tactics and hard work.

When you are given a task, instead of taking the plunge to start the task, begin by thinking about the task, then do not be afraid to ask as many good questions as you need to. This will save you an astonishing amount of time and effort. This can also save you from frustration. Do you agree that it can be quite frustrating to complete the task almost halfway only to find out that your original ideas about the task were not thorough enough?

Do not ignore the quid pro quo.

We do not usually like to talk about it, but the truth is that a quid pro quo is innate to all relationships. As mentioned earlier, quid pro quo means that something is always exchanged in return for something else. There are times when the quid pro quo is quite evident like when you sign an employment contract wherein your employer will pay you salary and in return, you will be expected to perform your job competently. However, there are instances when the quid pro quo is more indirect or subtle like "I will recommend you for promotion, and in return, I expect you to prioritize processing my transactions." A quid pro quo is a bartering system that normally remains unspoken in both relationships and organizations. Unfortunately, some people are not very adept at taking advantage of the quid pro quo. Instead of capitalizing on it, they freely give away favors to other people while expecting very little or nothing at all in return.

You can build better relationships when you identify the quid pro quo. Determine what you have that other people need or want, and decide what other people have that you need or want in return. Always remind yourself that every time you offer something to other people, you have earned something in return from them. The secret is to keep an account of those good deeds so you can have something to turn to when the right time comes. It is important that you always interact with other people with generosity of spirit.

This may sound deceitful to you, but you actually do this every day without even realizing it. For instance, you agreed to finish a report for a co-worker who had to leave early to attend her child's school performance. A couple of weeks later, you realize that that co-worker can help you with a particular task, and your colleague willingly helped you complete your task as a way of paying you for the favor you gave her before.

Here are some useful tips for you:

- When you have gone out of your way to help other people, make sure that they know about it. Naturally, be subtle about this.

- Do not let tasks appear very easy to complete. You can say something like: "I am pleased to tell you that I have finally convinced the technician to prioritize repairing your laptop so you will not need to wait for one week to get it. I knew you need it repaired before your out-of-town trip on Friday."

- Do not undervalue the barter value of even minor things like vocally giving your support to a colleague during a meeting or giving a public praise to a co-worker, or patiently listening to someone who wants to rant or even grapevine info.

- Get your return favors carefully but do not be afraid to get them. When you need someone to help you with an important task, do not be afraid to remind them of how you helped them in the past.

Do not allow other people to waste your time.

Have you ever experienced ending your day with a realization that you have not accomplished anything and one whole day was wasted because of other people? Right in the middle of your task, a colleague may go to your desk to ask something. Once you have returned to your work, you receive a call from another colleague seeking your advice. When this constantly happens to you, you need to always remind yourself that your time is one of your most valuable assets, and once you have lost it, you can never get it back.

I know that we are supposed to be kind and nurturing, but you need to realize that being kind and nurturing should not take precedence over being protective of your precious time. Before you address other people's concerns, make sure your own concerns have been adequately taken care of. Just like on a plane ride, put on your oxygen mask first before you attempt to help other people.

On the other hand, understand that I am not telling you to never make time for other people. When you do this, you will only cause irreparable damages to your relationships, which create many obstacles in the future. Instead, simply remain cognizant about how you let other people to exploit your precious time, particularly when you have none to give away.

Here are some tips on how you can prevent other people from wasting your time:

- Define the times when other people can approach you to discuss matters. Also define which urgent matters you can immediately attend to and which matters can be handled at a later time.

- Here is a sample statement you can give colleagues who have the habit of interrupting your work: "You know, I really would love to discuss this with you, but I am working on a very tight schedule today. I would appreciate if we can continue this discussion at 9am tomorrow."

- Keep piles of papers on the extra chairs in your office to prevent people from sitting down and having lengthy discussion with you when you need to concentrate on your own work.

- Do not put your pen down when a colleague enters your room.

- Set aside a specific time for answering phone calls, voice mails and emails. Give this schedule to your colleagues so they can expect when they can receive a reply from you. When someone constantly ignores the boundaries you have set, simply enforce it by saying "I really would love to talk to you but I just can't do it now."

- If you need to concentrate 100 percent, you can opt to put a "Please do not disturb" sign on your door.

- If someone else keeps you waiting for more than 20 to 30 minutes for a scheduled meeting, simply leave.

Chapter 4: Change How You Sound

Even your brightest ideas can fall on deaf ears if you cannot communicate them confidently and credibly. The message you have to deliver is irrelevant to the way you sound. Instead, the words that you choose, the tone of your voice, the pace of your speech and the organization of your thoughts affects how people hear what you are trying to say. All of these elements contribute to how knowledgeable, skilled and confident you appear to other people.

Do not express your statements as questions.

This is a very common error people make: thinking that asking a question is a safer way to express their opinions and ideas without appearing aggressive or pushy. Are you in the habit of saying starting your statements with "what would you think if we..." or "what do you think about...?" When you ask a question instead of making a statement, you give up ownership of your opinions and ideas and their potential outcomes.

If you are concerned about sounding harsh or aggressive, you can opt to add language to your statement to can make it more amenable – but stop yourself from converting your statements to questions at all costs. Every time you catch yourself doing it, stop talking and immediately transform your question to a statement. Keep your questions for those legitimate times when you truly need to obtain information from other people or when you are honestly seeking their opinion. To avoid sounding pushy, you can opt to add "I would like to hear your thoughts" at the end of your statement. This will make you more straightforward without appearing unsure of your own opinions.

Avoid using a preamble.

A preamble is basically a mixture of both non-words and words that are used prior to getting straight to the point. A preamble can actually be compared to a cluttered closet. When your closet is full of clutter, you no longer know what is in there. This applies to your words. If you use too many words, you are diluting the importance of the message you want to convey. This can prevent your listener from hearing what you want to communicate.

People normally employ a preamble as a technique of moderating their messages because they are afraid that they will be seen as very pushy or aggressive. Here are useful techniques you can use to be more straightforward when communicating:

- Start with your bottom line. Make sure that your thoughts are already organized prior to opening your mouth. You can do this by asking these two basic questions: "what is the main topic I want to discuss?" and "which specific points do I wish my listener to grasp or consider?"

- Always keep in mind that "concise sounds confident". If you truly believe your message is important, take the time to practice delivering it beforehand. Try refining your message by saying it with as few words as you can.

Avoid lengthy explanations.

The preamble has a counterpart and that is the long-winded explanation. This happens when ultimately you have made your point but then weaken it with an overly long explanation that causes your audience to leave you mentally. Combining a preamble with a lengthy explanation can truly be fatal to your communication. Why do people still make this mistake? One of the reasons is that people tend to believe that the more words they say, the more softened and acceptable their message will be. Another reason is that they believe the more words they say, the more powerful they appear. People are also afraid that they have not been in-depth or exhaustive enough, so they continue to talk. People also tend to give lengthy explanations when their audience does not acknowledge the given information. These people keep on talking in an effort to obtain a reaction from their audience. Lastly, people over explain to try compensating for their insecurities. They believe that the longer they talk, the better their argument becomes. They do not realize that the opposite is actually true.

Here are some tips you can use to avoid giving lengthy explanations:

- Always try to compress your explanations by 50 to 70 percent.

- After you have given your point, use only up to two or three additional details as follow up. Then tell yourself to stop. If you are waiting for an acknowledgement from your audience, your silence will become your audience's cue to give their reactions.

- Fight the self-conscious feeling that your explanation is incomplete. Always remind yourself that it is not necessary for you to say everything you know about the topic you are discussing. There are instances when you think that your explanation is incomplete, but in reality, it is already complete to your audience. Always remember that less is more.

You do not always have to ask for permission.

Successful people do not normally ask for permission. Instead, they ask for forgiveness after the fact. Some people always ask for permission before speaking their mind out of habit. This bad habit is actually a variation of expressing your statements as questions, but it is even more self-defeating. In our modern society, children are expected to ask for permission but adults are no longer expected to do it. Every time you ask permission to speak your mind, you diminish your stature and demote yourself to the position of a small child. You also set yourself up to hear a "no" answer. It may be true that when you seek permission before you act, you are less likely to be blamed for any mistakes, but you will likely be perceived as an insecure person who doesn't take risks.

No matter what your position is right now, always remember that you are entitled to act in the ways that you deem necessary and appropriate. Of course, keep in mind the limitations of your workplace. Determine what those limitations are, clear them up with your superiors and take actions within those limitations. Your superior wants you to succeed at your job, so he or she will be happy to help you.

- Instead of asking permission, inform the other parties of what your intentions. When you inform them, you are showing respect for their need to be informed, but not letting your action become conditional upon their approval.

- Transform your uncertain questions into confident statements. "Will it be possible for me to work from home tomorrow because I need to be there for the delivery that I expect around midday" sounds insecure. "I just wanted to inform you that I will be working from home tomorrow so I can accept the delivery I am expecting around midday" sounds self-assured.

- Work under the assumption that if other people have problems with what you are telling them, they will inform you. When you work from that assumption, you maintain a position with more power and strength.

- If you find it hard to use an affirmative declaration, you can make your message softer by giving a follow-up statement. Instead of asking for permission, you can say "I am planning to prepare a manual that the department can use as a guide to addressing the concerns of our customers. After I have completed the manual, I will forward it to you so you can give me your inputs and comments prior to releasing it to the whole department."

- You are asking a genuine question when you ask for data or information that you do not have or do not know. You can certainly ask this kind of question as long as you do not hold your audience hostage to your questions. Always mind the body language of the people you talk to, so you notice when you need to let them go. When this happens, you can save your other questions for a later time.

Do not apologize.

Tiger Woods was interviewed after losing in the British Open tournament wherein an interviewer mentioned that it was indeed a bad day for Tiger Woods because he missed a number of easy shots and played below his normal standards. Tiger Woods replied to those statements by saying, "I didn't play poorly. The wind and the conditions were just against me today."

You can take a lesson from Tiger Woods' statement. Apologizing for your low-profile and unintentional errors can erode your self-esteem and, consequently, erode other people's confidence in you. Do you profusely apologize when you bump into someone while walking on the street or when you make a minor mistake at work? To some people, apologizing seems to be second nature to them, and it is normally done instead of tackling the real source of the error or mistake, which is sometimes the poor communication of the other party. Apologizing can be considered as a technique used to reduce conflicts, but be aware that apologizing can make you look guilty or mistaken when you are actually not.

You will feel more empowered when you stop apologizing for every little error that you make. If you think that you have the bad habit of always apologizing, the first step is to begin tallying the number of times you needlessly apologize to other people. Do this deliberately everyday with the conscious intention of reducing the number by choosing to save your apologies for those mistakes that truly matter.

When you have made an error or mistake that is worth apologizing for, say your apologies only once and then immediately shift to the problem-solving stage. Transform your tendency to apologize into an objective evaluation of what has gone wrong and how you can fix them. Also stop yourself from apologizing in a manner that puts you in a weakened position in order to ensure the other party still likes you. Always start from a position of equality irrespective of the position of the person you are apologizing to. You may need to apologize to your boss or to someone who holds a higher position, but this does not mean the other person is any better compared to you.

Do not use minimizing words.

Minimizing words are those that weaken the value or the magnitude of your accomplishments. People normally use minimizing words to downplay their success and achievements by attributing them to something else instead of their own talents, hard work and expertise. How do you respond to people who congratulate and compliment you? Have you caught yourself saying things like: "Oh, it was really nothing" or "I think I just got lucky?" When you say those things all the time, you end up believing them yourself.

Here are useful tips on how to stop using minimizing words:

- Get into the habit of saying "thank you" when you are congratulated or complimented. You can practice saying it on your own so it will feel automatic when the time comes to say it to another person.

- Be objective when you describe your accomplishments. Avoid using qualifiers such as "I just...," "it was only..." or "I surprised even myself..."

- If you wish to be modest, you can say something like "Thank you. I am pleased with my achievement, but I need to give some recognition to the people who provided assistance along the way."

Conclusion

Thank you again for purchasing this book!

I hope this book helped you to understand how you can become more assertive and self-confident in dealing with your personal and work relationships.

The next step is to start practicing the lessons you have learned.

Thank you and good luck!